Dating Advice For Women

The Blueprint To Get The Perfect Man. Learn The Best Dating Secretes, Expert Tips & Capture Your Perfect Match!

Table of Contents

Introduction

I want to thank you for purchasing this book, *'Dating Advice For Women: Blueprint For The Perfect Man.'* Specially designed to help my fellow ladies with dating, this book has been carefully put together and meticulously written.

Times are tough. We stand in the 21st century, where definitions are changing and its updates are fast replacing solidified notions of love. We are a confused bunch. Our one leg is stuck in the baby-boomers' generation, while the other one wants to step into the millennials' era. We are somewhere straddling in between.

Additionally, at the outset, let me make this clear that this book is for the fairer sex. It aims at providing the womenfolk all the essential tips for dating and finding their true love. This book tries to explain what men really want from their women and how a basic understanding of their needs can go a long way in making dating for women swifter and easier.

Let us begin our journey without further ado.

Chapter 1: The Dynamics Of A Relationship

A typical relationship is forged between a male and a female, wherein they agree to love, support and stand by each other. It basically consists of two people who are madly in love. A modern day romantic relationship is touted to be weaker than a rather conventional relationship. However, that is a story for another chapter altogether. Let us study in detail the various dynamics that go into the operation of a modern day relationship.

Socioeconomic Factor

A lot depends on where the two partners are in their lives. It does not make sense for a person working a low paying job to fall for a person earning millions. Not only does it defy common sense, but it also violates a certain social code that has been largely followed when it comes to romantic relationships. One must fall for someone who is either lower than or equal in social stature. If you are a seeker, the above rule applies to you all the more.

It is the stuff of grand movies where the protagonist falls for a person way beyond his or her league and ends up achieving enough success to justify being with the concerned person. Let us snap back to real life, where socioeconomic status dictates a good chunk of one's dating life. Think about it? It matters how much money you make a month. In fact, a lot of romantic relationships derive themselves out of professional relationships, wherein people have a fair idea about the income status of each other. There are exceptions but this is a general rule of thumb to follow.

Imagine walking downtown to a fancy restaurant with your date. You have your food, spend some quality time admiring the interior and order dessert in the end. However, when the bill comes, it runs into thousands - something you had not anticipated. Imagine being red-faced in such a situation. Your date may not express it outrightly, but he/she will be feeling second-hand embarrassment too. If you do not belong to a particular earning bracket, make sure you struggle enough to be in it.

Even if you happen to be a woman, you cannot just expect your date to be making all the payments, especially in this day and age. That would be too shallow of you. Be an independent woman and have the potential to split bills whenever you go out.

Personality Types

No relationship is the result of the coming together of two random individuals with opposite personality types. A relationship is like a lock-and-key system. What one lacks the other must have. However, when it comes to personalities, a typical relationship requires the people involved to fall in love first. In order for that to happen, they must first be attracted toward each other. Attraction results from the matching of personalities of two individuals.

There are various personality types, ranging from extrovert to introvert and beyond. All that matters is which personality type suits yours. In order to find that out, you must "experiment" a lot. It is not easy to fit in with every available personality type.

Aspiration

Every woman wants to "settle" for the right guy. In today's world, women are vocal about what they want and where they want to be in life. Dating is not simply an activity that exists in a vacuum. Who you date also affects other aspects of your life. For example, maybe you want to see yourself as the managing partner of your firm in the next two years.

Now this dream of yours may not have any connection to your dating life, but eventually, it will. Your professional front will subsequently get affected by your personal one. Who you date has a good impact on how your aspirations are going to pan out in the next couple of years. Hence, it becomes vital, in such a scenario, to choose wisely! Appearances can be deceiving!

Chemistry

You cannot find a comfort level with every single person that you meet. A certain amount of chemistry must be there in a couple for it to keep happening. If a couple that has no spark at the beginning of a relationship, it is very likely that the relationship will perish soon.

Whether chemistry exists between two people or not is decided largely by third-party onlookers. They are the best judge of the presence or lack of chemistry between two people since they are not blinded by romantic feelings or lust. But can view each relationship objectively and factually.

Psychology of Men

Men need attention too. Sex is only a small component of a relationship, men want something more such as, being spoiled by your maternal characteristics. They want to be cared for, accepted and want their egos inflated. Men are very simple creatures when it really boils down to it. All you need to do is understand how they tick.

Satisfying their sexual desires is just one piece of the puzzle, and believe it or not men want something more than just "physical pleasure", they truly want to have companionship! Someone who can make them laugh, support their endeavors, someone to take care of them when they become ill, someone to cook for them and ultimately someone to grow old with, and lastly someone they can protect and cherish the moment with.

Chapter 2: Maternal Characteristics Men Look For

Men were traditionally hunters. Their sole objective was to hunt and hunt as fast as possible because the children back in the cave were not going to wait forever for their mothers to make them a scrumptious meal. So you see - men are hardwired to be objective by nature.

While women, on the other hand, get to be picky because they were the ones who gathered the spices and herbs and they had to be particularly careful about this because if they were not, then poisonous mushrooms could really cause them a lot of inconvenience.

Hence keeping all this in mind, it is safe to assume that men are hardwired to also expect a certain set of qualities from their potential life partners.

Caring

Care stems from your ability to be empathetic and sympathetic as well. If your little one gets his knees bruised during a basketball game and the dad is away working overtime or cracking open a cold one at Billy's, it is time for mama bear to take charge. A woman knows her stuff and she knows how to apply first aid and stay by her son until he is fine. Care is an essential trait, one that cannot be overlooked in any healthy relationship.

Care, after all, is a manifestation of the love you are both going to share. In my honest opinion, there is no other better way to show someone that you love them than plain honestly and earnestly caring for them with all your heart and soul. When you care for someone, it shows in your actions and inactions alike. So be careful and do not try to fake it as the effort is going to be futile. Make a habit out of it as it's a great one to have.

Men find this trait extremely attractive, and I myself do too from personal experience. Why? When your man gets sick, who does he have to turn to? When you take that opportunity to care and nurture him back to good health his love for you will grow, and it shows him affection and consideration for his ill condition. A man wants a woman who can look after him when he's at his lowest point in life, keep this in mind.

Helpful

I cannot remember when was the last time I managed to misplace something in my house and my mom was unable to find it for me. I also cannot remember the last time I asked my father to do the same for me. You see, regardless of who you are, you have certain expectations from the amazing women in your life, be it your mother or your life partner.

We trust our women to be helpful because if not them, then who else? We know that they will be our bright guiding stars in times of absolute darkness and desolation.

Some ladies might view this as a burden but, believe me, it's really a privilege in disguise. I am a man and God knows what I'd give away to commend that kind of goodwill, expectation and respect from my children. I am guessing a man can never compete with a woman in this domain. A woman is the true jack-of-all-trades and that is why this is one trait that you must, by all means possible, learn to incorporate into who you are.

Affectionate

The world does a number on a man in several different ways, every single day. His boss is being demanding beyond reason. His colleagues are a nasty lot and the monotony of the work and deadlines can be soul crushing. So once he is back home, he will expect someone to be there for him and undo all that damage and ugliness he has imposed upon himself throughout the day. The same applies for the child. The schools and the colleges aren't as green as they might seem. The world has a lot of unpleasantness in store to throw at us and permanently keep us down on our knees and it tends to get overwhelming sometimes.

In times such as these, you can only trust a lady to be your sole beacon of hope and reservoir of love, compassion and affection. The wounds need to be tended, and emotional support extended. It is no coincidence that a woman is considered a successful man's lucky charm.

Keep in mind that this is the absolute cornerstone of every relationship. Women look for characteristics of their father in their men and men look for the signs of their mother in their women. Affectation is a constant in the equation. It's essentially the sugar in the cake. Be generous in this regard and bake yourself a delicious one.

As mentioned above, men tend to search for the traits of their mothers in their women. They have been brought up in a certain way and conditioned in a particular manner ever since they were kids. Whatever qualities their mothers had have now left a good impression upon their minds. Such qualities may be entirely destructive or wholly beautiful. They will always be one of the criteria by which men judge a woman.

However, the traits so elucidated in this chapter are some of the universally accepted maternal traits that must warrant their presence in a woman's nature for a man to be attracted towards her.

Chapter 3: The Need For Distance

Now I don't want to let this title mislead you in creating extreme distance between you and your partner, but allow your significant other to go out with his friends, don't constantly check up on him, text him and ask him excessive questions, there needs to be a degree of trust.

Absence makes the heart yearn, what you see in Hollywood movies is not realistic, being with your partner 24/7 living happily ever after. Minus the happily ever after part, it's just not possible to be in constant contact and communication with your partner all throughout the day.

You both have your lives to live, and I've seen it way too often, relationships falling apart or deteriorating because partners get bored of each other! How much can you really talk about 24/7 365 days a year?

You'd be driven insane and quite easily become bored. Absence is a normal part of a relationship, and if one partner is too "clingy" this is a sign of insecurities and can lead to "breaking up". This phenomenon is all too well played out and documented in lives of celebrities, they have all the money you could dream of, freedom to go anywhere they want, buy anything they desire, designer clothes, dream mansions, and yet most "Hollywood relationships" simply do not last. Why? Simply because of "boredom" due to fact of seeing each other too often, hence you see the phenomenon of short term and polygamist sort of relationships/lifestyles.

A friend of mine happened to be in a long distance relationship and it was all sunshine.Things were going great and they rarely had any misunderstandings. According to him, it was a beautiful relationship and he felt that it was only the beginning. He was hopeful that the future had great things in store for both of them and, once they were together, it would only get better and better.

Sadly they broke up, which seemed pretty normal considering that this is the fate most relationships suffer, until I realized that they broke up hardly a month after he relocated to her town. This was a relationship where years were invested. So what went wrong? If a relationship could fare so well despite the distance, why did it collapse when the distance was taken out of the equation?

We all have the answer, we know it, but we are just not willing to or ready to admit it. We love our significant other and we are so passionate about that person, so much so that sometimes it tends to suffocate you to a point of total madness. We do not realize it because we are blinded by our love. We are so starry-eyed that we don't see ourselves tripping over our shoelaces and going down the rabbit hole.

This one is a bitter pill to swallow but it is one that you need to face. The problem must be acknowledged and dealt with. An moderate amount of distance must be maintained and exercised for the survival and sustenance of your relationship. Sometimes, he just wants to watch dumb action movies without being judged while burying his face in a bag of Cheetos and gulping down the 20th can of cold beer. It's not a pretty sight and he just wants to be left alone in his man-cave. - ok maybe this is a little bit of an exaggerated example, but you get the picture!

A man is owed his indulgence. It takes a lot of mental fortitude to act civilized all the time. He is not cheating on you. He is recharging himself for your sake. Ever kept a shirt locked up in a damp cupboard for too long? Chances are it started to stink. Or even better yet, here is an analogy below to keep in mind.

You have a butterfly in your hand which signifies your relationship, and what most people tend to do is have an excessive strong grip or clenched fist on the butterfly. This will suffocate and eventually destroy the butterfly. Now let's keep this in context, imagine your relationship, this strong grip represents the constant clinginess to see each other and desire to be together. The appropriate course of action is to hold the butterfly in your hands with a hold that is gentle allowing the butterfly its freedom to go and come back as it pleases.

The beauty of the message here is your significant other must have the freedom to "fly" and depart, and only when this freedom is given your significant other will return to that which he now considers home (with YOU). Do you see the simplicity and beauty of that analogy, do not suffocate relationships with constant clinginess, and allow for time away from each other to recharge, reflect and recuperate. Absence makes the heart yearn remember that, so it would make sense to create a moderate amount of distance when necessary, hang out with your other friends, etc.

The same rule applies to our relationships. Keep your significant other chained to a leash like an animal and he will grow irritable and upset. Set him free and he is bound to come back to you guaranteed. We are, after all, a species that has fought wars for freedom.

Freedom is an entitlement and it can be achieved in any relationship by knowing what the personal boundaries of the said person are. Understand when the other person wants his space. Respect him enough to trust him and believe that he will not misuse your faith. Good relationships can only exist between two independent individuals.

Chapter 4: The Element of Trust

Hard to earn and even harder to maintain, trust is like China; once broken, it becomes very difficult to piece together. The glue is going to hold the pieces together, but the cracks still show.

You had a great beginning, a connection, a match of wavelengths, you've both been caught stealing glances and it feels good in his company. Now comes the dreaded time of letting your guard down and allowing yourself to be the dreaded bulletproof jacket. "I told her about getting drunk last night but didn't mention that I almost called my ex. It was after all out of a habit, not a will to get back with her. But must I tell her?" "Should I tell her Rebecca's been hitting on me? She hasn't told me who's been hitting on her."

Can you trust your partner with such information? It sometimes becomes a mind-numbing decision. So how do you tackle such a situation? Easy. You do not. You go ahead and share. You share and share and share until your heart bleeds dry and there's not much left to share. Honesty matters.

Before demanding trust from your partner, step back for a moment and ask yourself, "If I am looking for trust in my partner, is it not fair to assume he too is looking for the same?" The answer to this question, before leading you to seek reasons to trust your partner, forces an introspecting gaze and the ever-pounding question "Am I trustworthy?" "Have I given in return what I seek from my partner?"

Trust is something you need to earn. You cannot simply expect your partner to start having blind faith in you from the very beginning. Simple acts of love and care are what finally work towards creating trust bit by bit. It takes a good amount of time to be able to trust. People who can easily trust are highly likely to enter into bad relationships.

Trust few and trust well. It is a healthy practice to not trust someone easily. Not only does this save you from getting disappointed in the case of betrayal, but it also invites him to gain your trust. This procedure of 'gaining your trust' leads to a partner showering his attention and love on you. When extended and prolonged, such a process leads to ultimate happiness and bonding between the two partners.

What to do when there's lack of trust?

If there is a lack of trust between you and your partner, you need to work on it. Lack of trust usually results from a person's inherent inability to easily trust someone or some bad experience that must have wiped out any amount of trust the person chose to have. Either way, trust suffers and it's unhealthy for the relationship that suffers severe blows because of this. The absence of trust or lack thereof is like a leech that sticks on to a healthy limb and slowly sucks the blood out of the body.

When people are not able to trust each other, it separates them in the long run. Not only do they start becoming unaware of what the other partner is up to, but they also begin to shut themselves down completely. Such a dual blow on a person who is in a relationship is harmful and must be dealt with from its very roots. The root causes of the absence of trust have been mentioned above. You cannot change the fundamental nature of an individual.

However, it needs to be mentioned here that people who distrust a lot are the same people whose trust, once gained, will be concrete and will last a long time. The trust so gained from distrusting people is made out of strong stuff and lasts a long while. Hence, the absence or lack of trust is not entirely a bad thing. I know it sounds a little complicated but it isn't really when you take time to sit on it and digest.

Trust is said to be broken on account of many things. It could be because of that one time when she found a lipstick mark on the collar of your shirt, or all the times you keep checking your phone too often. It is easy for some people to start suspecting others. You cannot dispute the fact that, in a relationship, it is a natural thing to be protective of your partner.

It is very human to be aware of all the attention that is being showered upon your partner from the opposite sex. You should not feel guilty about feeling insecure regarding your partner. On the other hand, it is the mark of a good relationship that you are harboring feelings of insecurity with regard to your partner. The more the level of insecurity, the stronger the love between you two is. In international relation terms, the more precious the ambassador is, the tighter the security around him becomes.

It is hence very natural for you to feel that way. However, you tend to cross the line when you start distrusting your partner on account of such feelings of the mentioned insecurity. It is utterly unfair to your partner that he/she has to suffer because of some ill-founded thoughts that happened to cross your mind.

A common mistake that people end up making when dealing with a lack of trust in their relationship is limiting the scope of potential trust in the future. Lack of trust is not dealt with by a further lack of trust. That is a sure shot way to make sure whatever small amount of trust there is between the both of you to be reduced to zero. The solution is not a further division between the two of you.

The solution is to amicably sit down and discuss the issues going on between you. A good conversation works wonders in a dying relationship. Furthermore, by talking, you make sure that whatever misunderstandings or confusions both of you have are at least addressed. A lot of issues in relationships do not get addressed in the first place. It is very important that you acknowledge that there exists problems in your relationship. It is only after this accepting of the problems that you will be able to move forward to solve them.

Why is Trust Important?

Trust is the very cement of a relationship. It is one of the fundamental foundations upon which a relationship is built. A relationship is like dancing. You have to accept some things and take a leap of faith in order to perform well. You have to trust your partner to pick you up when you fall and catch you when you blindly take a fall. Just like dancing, your partner and you must always be in synchronization.

The element of trust in a relationship is of primary importance to you because, without it, the relationship is next to nothing. Until both the partners have learned to have blind faith in each other, the relationship would be considered to be in its initial nascent stage. That being said, it not easy for some people to just blindly trust someone they have just entered into a relationship with.

Due to past experiences or just the way the world goes, it is becoming next to impossible to even fathom trusting a random stranger who vows to keep you happy. But, trust is such a crucial element that once gained, could take a relationship to amazing new levels. It assures both the partners of the strength of the bond that exists between you and keeps you from suspecting the basis of your relationship.

As has been mentioned a billion times before now, trust is really difficult to gain. It is more valuable than diamonds, and once gained, it must be guarded with your life. Under no account let the trust you have gained from your partner go to waste. As long as you keep holding on to the trust element of your relationship, regardless of how much you two fight or argue, the relationship is there to stay. Incredible right?

Maintaining Trust

Once consolidated, trust is a cakewalk to maintain. It is the building up of the trust that takes real time and effort. However, once you have gained the trust of your partner, all you have to do to keep it in that very same condition is to water it every day. It is like raising a fruit-giving tree in your backyard. Your job does not stop at simply planting the seed in the soil. You have to nourish it like a parent. You have to provide it with sunlight, nutrients, manure, the proper amount of water and everything that helps a seed develop into a sapling and then subsequently a huge tree that gives you juicy fruits.

Though the act of maintaining the gained trust is easy, you must not forget to water the seed daily. Small acts of affection like calling now and then to ask about their whereabouts go a long way toward making sure that the seed you had planted is growing. Do not, under any circumstance, take the matter of trust lightly. Remember that your partner is important to you and they deserve the best out of you. Your efforts in the direction of not just gaining their trust but also keeping it count as the best thing you can give someone you love.

Have you ever seen builders spray water on newly poured concrete? Get the idea now? You've put concrete in the form of trust. How do you maintain the strength after repeated shockwaves from everyday life? Communication is your water. Saying, "I trust you" does wonders. It reinforces a bond and the gullible heart melts. Moreover, if your partner was uncertain about sharing something, these three words would go a long way to make him feel sure about his decision.

Or if he's been hiding something, his guilt radar will start beeping like it happens with a stolen vehicle. They'll realize their mistake without you pointing it out so you get no drama, and gain brownie points. One stone, two birds. Amazing right?

Share your future plans and make him a part of all major events of your life with actions if not possible in words. The last thing you want is for him to find out an embarrassing thing about you from another source. And boy, that escalates the awkwardness of explanations. It is better that your partner hears about that close-bodied tango with Rebecca from you with a few chuckles than from the mouth of an evil sprouting devil of a friend. The human mind goes to the dark side in an instant and finding the way back can be quite a task if help is not offered.

But what to do when your partner is angry with you and feeling betrayed? How do you regain the lost trust? How do you claim a second chance? What steps do you need to take to make up and realize your mistakes? Brace yourself; it's going to be tough. A smile or a gift is not going to help this time. What's going to go a long way is sincerity and perseverance. Convincing a partner who doesn't wish to be convinced is like making him let go of a habit. Difficult at first, and time-consuming later. With the right amount of space and the right mix of investment of time and emotion, trust can be maintained and regained.

So if you've messed up, get ready to clean it up, and apply a fresh layer of concrete. Unless you do that, you don't have the right to tell yourself you gave it your best shot.

Chapter 5: Essential Ingredients Of A Relationship

Talking about the fundamentals of a relationship, you must first set out with a clear goal in mind. You do not have to impress your man; you have already done that. That's the reason why he is with you in the first place. You two are in a relationship already. Your work involves banking upon the impression you have made.

You should capitalize on the merits upon which your partner has chosen to stay with you and continues to cohabitate with you. This chapter is all about all the key elements that actually play a vital role in building, maintaining and sustaining a relationship.

First and foremost, you need to have a certain level of respect towards your partner. It has already been established that both of you decided to be in a relationship and such a decision was a mutual one. That means your partner has put a great deal of faith in you to treat him with respect and love. While love is easy to give, respect comes with difficulty. When you respect your partner, it sends a message that is loud and clear: You do not take him for granted. Most relationships falter at the initial stages because one of the partners realizes that the other partner doesn't really respect them.

It is this difference in the behavior pre and post relationship that appalls them and forces them to have second thoughts about coming into a relationship with you. Respect becomes difficult to give when you are in a relationship that involves a lot of arguments and fights. It is your duty to keep your mind clear. You cannot afford to cross the threshold of anger when you are in a conflict with your partner.

Remember, this threshold, when crossed, can lead you to form a habit of losing your cool with your partner. You need to always keep in mind that your partner, regardless of how much he is contributing to the relationship, is a human being and deserves the same respect that you expect from him. Respecting your partner also makes you appreciate his point of view even when you are fighting. Being able to see the other side's point of view is a rare occurrence in relationships these days.

The second thing that must be kept in mind while trying to pay attention to the little things in a relationship is, as it has been mentioned above, the point of view of the opposite side. No relationship exists without its own share of fights. Every individual who has ever been in a relationship will relate to this.

Without the heated fights and long-drawn arguments, no relationship has ever been real. It is a hard-hitting reality to those who are new to a relationship that eventually fights and arguments are bound to happen. What you can do to minimize their adverse effects is make sure you are prepared for it. This preparation could be done in many ways. One of the top ways is to be ready to accept the point of view of the other party. Point of view can be best described as the reference point through which the other party is speaking.

It is basically about being in the shoes of the other person and seeing things from their perspective. We often tend to ignore the point of view of those people who are against us. Anyone disagreeing with us tends to get blocked and we simply refuse to even consider their perspective of the whole issue. When this happens in a relationship, it tends to isolate one partner from the other. Be willing to accept the views of your partner despite how revolting or absurd they may sound. It does not hurt to at least lend him your ear. You are free to disagree or contest his opinions but without even first receiving his perspective, you cannot expect to form your judgment on the subject.

Thirdly, we forget to love after a while in a relationship. The love you shower upon your partner long after you get into a relationship with him differs from the love you used to display during your courtship days. This difference should not be too much. When this difference is large, it is usually considered to be bad for a relationship.

For example, if you used to drive all the way from your workplace to your partner's workplace during lunch hours, just so you could spend time together during the break, and now you don't even share one meal of the day in the same place, it is a sure indicator of love fading away. It so happens that after getting into a relationship, most people take things for granted. It is this, taking things for granted, that makes him forget the most important element of the relationship which should be love. Never forget to show your partner that you still love him the same way you used to during your initial days.

Small tokens of love like bringing home flowers while on your way back home, or surprising him with a candlelight dinner or taking your partner out for a suddenly planned movie; these are all examples of how you can keep reminding your partner about the love between the two of you burning with the same ferocity and intensity. Do not forget to be the same person you were before the relationship happened. If you change drastically after coming into a relationship, your partner is going to find it offensive and unpleasant.

However, all said and done, one cannot deny the inevitable fact that change does creep in after a relationship is affected between two individuals. Things take a more serious course and ultimately start establishing themselves in a more concrete manner. In order to avoid changes turning into drastic changes, you can choose to do away with the extra burdens that come along with a new relationship. Do not let the difficulties of a new relationship overshadow what you had before.

Fourthly, have a lot of conversation. We do a lot of things for our better halves. From getting them their favorite dress from the costliest of companies to taking them out for dinners- we leave no stone unturned when it comes to pleasing our partners. What we tend to ignore in all of this is the importance of a simple conversation. When was the last time you sat together on the front porch and had a really nice talk about things in general?

When was the last time you guys dined together only to find

yourself engaging in a deep conversation about how your relationship needs a revival from the mundanity of things? The power of a conversation is often underestimated. What can be achieved by a good old conversation cannot be achieved by other displays of love and affection! The conversation you are having need not be about you. It could be about anything in general.

For example, you could discuss the general elections of the year, exchange views about feminism or talk about the future of your school-going kid. A conversation, regardless of whichever topic it deals with, is powerful enough to build back lost connections or damaged ones. It serves the purpose of successful articulation of thoughts and opinions.

Fifthly, give each other an ample amount of space. When you give your partner the right amount of space, it serves a dual purpose. It allows your partner the chance to have a private sphere of his/her own and secondly, it gives you the opportunity to do the same. Not every issue related to relationships can be dealt with getting closer than before. Sometimes, it is wiser to do the opposite. It is often considered the right step to take a step back and think through things. It is sometimes the right step to take when you distance yourself from your partner in order to develop and adopt a new perspective with regards to things that exist or do not exist between the two of you.

Another very important ingredient of a successful relationship that people overlook is honesty. Less and less people are being honest these days. When it comes to something as important as a relationship that rests on mutual understanding, honestly assumes a vital role. If you are being completely transparent with your partner, your relationship is going to survive for a long time.

However, on the other hand, if you tend to hide a few things here and there from your partner, chances are really high that slowly but surely, your relationship starts tumbling down the hill. Honesty need not be shown in all transparency. Being honest and being transparent are two different things altogether. Sometimes, you have to be a little dishonest in order to save your relationship by looking at the bigger picture.

If you are being entirely transparent with your partner, you are in for some serious trouble. A person cannot imagine sharing everything with his or her partner. Now that would be ridiculous to even suggest. There are always such things that we choose to keep hidden from our partners. Such things are best kept that way forever. Being honest does not mean that you tell your partner every single thing that occurred in your life or crosses your mind. You need to have a proper "filter" and discern what can be said and not. Kind of like how a water filter sifts out certain "waste products" (salts, dirt, etc) ie: information you do not want to share, and allows only "water" to pass through.

Become friends with your partner. A romantic relationship surely binds two individuals together and lets them share each other's bodies and minds like never before but it's the bond of friendship that really brings two people together. If you are able to establish a strong bond of friendship with your partner, you have successfully become their partner in the truest sense of the word. Your friendship needn't be tainted by the element of romance. In order for you to become a good friend, you must be able to understand your partner on a deep level. You should be not just an ally in his/her times of celebration but also a strong supporter in times of despair and need. Being a friend to your romantic partner is not easy. A relationship that has crossed the thresholds from being platonic is difficult sometimes. The stages of a relationship are usually pretty simple.

First comes the platonic relationship and then the romantic one. People who have successfully traveled through the platonic ones move ahead to the romantic ones. The platonic relationship is all about pure friendship. It is that stage of interaction between two individuals when they admire each other without getting attracted or falling in love. It is the bond of friendship that comes out to save your relationship when everything falls apart eventually. Being friends with a person gives you that license to know everything there is to know about them. You know exactly what makes them pleased and what repulses them.

Chapter 6: Insecurities

Insecurity isn't pretty and can easily destroy any relationship or prospects of a relationship. It always starts with rhetorical questions and personal investigations as you start to overthink everything that is possible. It has two stages: one where you start to question your partner and the next one where you start to question yourself.

This part of the book will teach you how to deal with insecurities. The cause of insecurity as well as its cure is something that resides within you. All you have to do is deal with the cause and work towards the cure.

The first step is to find out the cause of the insecurity - only when you address this will you be able to work on solving it.

What is the Cause?

We all have a past and old feelings that will continue to haunt us. Relationships and dating put us in a vulnerable position which forces out of all these distant hurts, which start to haunt us today.

Insecurity starts from the way that you attach yourself to another person. You develop your attachment style in a relationship depending on the person that you are dating. This attachment style influences how your relationship plays out. So, if you have a secure attachment then you will be confident and there will be a lack of insecurity in your relationship. If your attachment is anxious then you are more likely to feel insecure about things.

So, you need to recognize your attachment style for each relationship. This will help you to understand the dynamics of your relationship and what kind of people make you feel anxious. It'll also help to be familiar with things from the past that might be causing your insecurities. Lastly, it will help you to understand how your insecurity might be as a result of some old feelings, baggage or negative past experience instead of something in the present.

Dealing with Insecurity

You have to understand the thing that was causing the problem in the first place. You have to face that inner voice which continuously tells you to doubt things and question all actions.

Here are some helpful tips:

Maintain independence:
It doesn't matter if you are dating or in a relationship, you have to try to have a personality that is not dependent on your partner. This sense of self, which is independent, will allow you to feel more confident.

Don't act out:
Anxiety can make us do crazy things and the first rule to keep in mind is to never act out no matter how you are feeling.

You have to be patient; don't do things in haste because you might regret them later.

Don't seek reassurance:

You should not expect the person you're dating or are in a relationship with to reassure you every time you feel insecure. This just contributes to your circle of insecurity and you'll never learn to deal with it independently. Also this can deter your significant other from further developing this relationship.

Stop evaluating everything:

You need to calm your inner voice that tells you to doubt everything and question everyone. If you keep evaluating every move that your partner makes, you will eventually find something that will make you feel insecure.

Chapter 7: Dating Advice for Single Mothers

Everybody has some dating experience and as a single woman, I am sure you must have acquired some dating skills. So, it might seem easy to start again, this time as a single mother. But it's not going to be simple — you have to throw everything that you learned about dating as a single woman out of the window. Dating as a single mother is an absolutely different game, which has its own set of rules and procedures. There aren't any shortcuts for this process and this section will teach you everything you need to know about the dating world of single mothers.

Learn To Accept That You Are Single

Losing a partner isn't easy at all and it takes an emotional as well as a mental toll on you. It doesn't matter why you lost your partner but the first thing that you need to do is move on and receive closure. It's going to be impossible to date other people if you can't accept the fact that you are single and that you need someone.

The first step is learning to emotionally deal with what happened — go to therapy or talk to someone. Being single isn't easy and many people continue to stay connected to their past. This won't bode well for you if you try to date another person because you won't be able to connect with them. You have to be emotionally available in order to ensure that you have a fair chance of connecting with someone else.

So, take some time out after you become single and learn to accept what happened. Only after you have done this will you genuinely be able to step into the dating world and will start to see better results.

Maturity

Dating a single mother requires you to be extremely mature because the margin of error for you is zero. You have kids and you're going to bring whoever you date into their lives. You have to balance what you want with what is best for your kids. So, you have to handle every date with maturity in order to make sure that you don't make any decision that you might regret later on.

The best way to do this is to be patient — don't make any decision without thinking twice about it. This will help you to understand the consequences of what you are doing and you will be able to make better decisions.

Date Someone Who Gets Your Life

It isn't easy being a single mother and if you continue to date people who don't understand what you are going through then you'll never find someone worth going forward with. It's important in any relationship to have some level of association — it helps you to connect with each other and to understand the struggle that both of you are going through.

It is even more important for people who are single and have kids because the struggle for them is tougher. You need someone who understands what you're going through, someone who can help you in your life and can relate to your struggle.

The ideal situation is to date someone who also happens to be single and has kids as well. It will be easier for you to connect with such a person and you will be more comfortable around them.

Ask more Questions before a Date

I know that it is tough being single and you want to jump into dating as soon as possible but you have to be careful. Dating isn't easy these days because of the various ways there are to get dates. It's impossible to know what a person is like if you just talk to them on a dating app. So, ask as many questions as you possibly can before you go out on a date to ensure that you don't make things difficult for yourself.

A bad date can be a horrible and traumatic experience, which many people don't recover from. It can scare you enough to have inhibitions about any future dating prospects. It is better to be careful from the start so that such a thing doesn't happen instead of trying to deal with it later.

It's also important to be honest about yourself when you're dating. Tell the person everything about your situation so that they have the option of stepping away if they feel uncomfortable.

Must like Kids

You can't compromise when it comes to kids; the person that you are dating has to be okay with the fact that you have kids. If they have any sort of problem with it then no matter how much you like them, they won't be worth it.

Being okay with the fact that you're dating someone who has kids can be a little difficult to swallow for many especially, if the person you are dating is from a younger generation and has no experience at all when it comes to dealing with kids. You are going to bring this person into your life and by extension, into your kid's lives. You have to make sure that your kids aren't left out of the decision-making process when you're dating someone.

Expect Resistance from your Kids

You are going to bring someone new into your kid's lives so you should not expect them to be positive about it. They will have some problems but you should try to talk it out with them. Firstly, be honest with them about the fact that you are seeing someone so that they can get used to that idea. You should sit them down and explain to them that you need someone in your life just like they need friends.

It won't be easy because kids don't tend to think maturely

about all of this. They had you all to themselves and now they have to share, the natural reaction for them would be to resist this. But, with time, they will be able to understand if you keep talking to them. Remember that, at the end of the day, it's your life and you have to make the decisions and not your kids.

Single Mother Perk/Advantage

Do not view your circumstance of already having children prior to going into a relationship as "baggage". You are unique and deserve someone who will appreciate your different set of circumstances and what you have to offer. It is true "some" men may be deterred from pursuing any meaningful relationship if you already have had children, but the good news is there is a lot of men out there who will accept you for who you are, and thus focus on these men.

Capitalize on your assets, through your child rearing experiences you have gained a lot more valuable life experiences than that of your counterparts(single females without children), experiences they do not have! For example, having children has obviously taught you how to cook, budget expenses, posses self-discipline, and you are more likely to have stronger maternal qualities which attribute to you as a person. YOU have as much of an advantage as that of your counterpart females without children. Perhaps even more one could argue.

Chapter 8: Modern Dating For Women

The Internet has been a revelation of sorts. Right from providing you groceries at your doorsteps to helping you pick your favorite car at the click of a mouse, it has allowed you to experience the world while you sit at home, sipping coffee. When it comes to romance, the Internet has been equally helpful. More often than not, modern day romance stories bloom from the Internet. Tinder, Facebook, Plenty of fish (POF) etc have now replaced love letters. Let us get you familiar with all the dos and don'ts of online dating in brief.

Looks Aren't Everything

In this day in age we are so focused and caught up with body image, but believe it or not looks are not everything! Take a profile picture that shows you doing something intriguing and then update your interests to the maximum extent possible. If you can't be hot, you can compensate by being an interesting person at the very least.

The right man will take a winning personality over sexy appeal any day. Here are some ideas, take pictures that show you reading a book, going on an adventure, at your favorite eatery or at the beach. Since Most dating apps focus on pictures you need to create an intriguing perception, and you must find the right way to leave behind a interesting impression based on your pictures alone. The old adage is true a picture is worth a thousand words!

Say Yes to All

Not to sound creepy, but it is the most practical advice a woman can use, especially when it comes to online dating through Tinder. Here is the logic behind it. Tinder works on the principle that unless both the parties swipe yes to each other, it does not give you a result. Swiping yes to every man that comes across your screen lets you have that far fetched shot at ending up getting paired with anyone who said yes to your picture. It is then entirely up to you to either reject the guy or accept him upon further conversation. It is not like you have signed a treaty or something, right?

By doing this you are working something called your "law of averages". I don't mean to get all statistical and technical on you, but here is some interesting facts on how the law of average works in a simplified sense, the more you match and say "yes" the more likely your going to match and find someone suitable on the dating app. Also as a woman you have a huge advantage when it comes to dating apps as 70-80% of guys on dating apps throw themselves at you! You won't even need to go seeking, they'll come right to you. How's that sound?

Don't play Hard to Get

The best thing about online dating is that it is casual in nature. Anyone who signs up for it is aware that they have done so for the purpose of indulging in some mingling by the end of it. No one is going to judge you for replying too fast or asking too many questions. This is a different form of online dating platform.! In such a scenario, it makes no sense to play hard to get. Do not wait hours before replying to look cool or important as that one message awaiting a response from you could be your potential significant other. If you wait too long, there are high chances of the guy not being interested in you anymore or moving on to someone else.

Make the first Move

As pointed out above, there are a million guys waiting to grab your current match the moment you starts paying attention to them! Your chances of developing some sort of social bond tends to expire in the following hour of the match being made if not kindled. Do not hesitate to send the first message fearing all the judgmental things the guy is going to think about you. He is probably not going to wait longer than a day for your reply.

Take Matters Offline

Once you have established good rapport with the man and think he is decent enough to meet over coffee or dinner even, then you should propose to take matters outside of social media. Mention how you rarely use the application and on one of such rare times you did use it, you happened to find him. A bit of harmless lying won't hurt. This establishes quite a few things in his mind, one you are not some "promiscuous girl" whom is looking for something temporary, two he is one of the lucky guys to have encountered you since you "do not" often use dating apps.

Also casually ask him if he would be interested in giving you his number for texting purposes. Bring the pace up, as this will make him realize that you are not one of the many profiles that he happened to come by. By proposing to take matters into the real world, you will be inducing the thought in his head that you are somewhat serious about taking matters further.

Don't feel Guilty

Research has pinpointed that the majority of women who take to online dating sites are those who have recently suffered through heartbreak. POF, Tinder and other similar apps are online platforms that play host to heartbroken people who are looking for a rebound. There will be times when you will feel guilty about being on Tinder only because you just broke up. There will be stages when you will feel like you are cheating on someone who dumped you. Do not let such moments take over. Remember, your past should not be allowed to dictate your present.

You just got out a relationship that was probably bad for you. Why else did it end? Dating provides you a good substitute for rebounding. It allows you to discover other fish in the sea while not feeling bad about it. Feeling guilty defeats the very purpose of using app-based dating. You deserve all the fun in the world if you are a woman who just got her heart broken. Feeling bad about it in phases is not going to help your situation at all. So chin up and go after the rest of the fish.

Chapter 9: You Are In Control

There is a certain balance that needs to be maintained. This balance exists between two polar opposites - Independence and Submissiveness. If you want your man to not feel intimidated by how independent you are, you must learn the art of being submissive when required. You do not have to compromise your principles in order to give in to a man's whims. All you need to do is play the game according to the weather.

An Independent Woman

An independent woman is a powerful woman. She knows the exact thing she wants and leaves no stones unturned to achieve it. She is sexually liberated and is quite vocal about her needs in bed. She won't stop at minor hurdles and appear weak in front of others. She will be fiercely competitive when required and quickly gentle when the circumstance so demands. An independent woman has all the qualities of a fighter. She can manage her work and home all at the same time and still find time for some recreational activities.

As a woman you need to understand YOU are in control. I've seen it with my own eyes women who are independent, focused and adventurous tend to be happier than their extremely submissive counterparts. Now, being submissive isn't a bad thing, however a men who sees the value of an independent women knows he has found something precious and will do everything in his strength to keep her. Why?

He knows he can be replaced, and a woman who's independent can also be the surrogate "leader" in the relationship. Ultimately there needs to be a balancing act between submission and Independence, you want to try to find the middle path, be too independent and some men may actually be intimidated, but be too timid or submissive and men may take advantage of you or simply may not be interested.

A Submissive Woman

This stereotype of woman is frowned upon in today's era of feminism. This lady is content with staying at home, preparing food for the family and tending to household chores throughout the day. She is humble, caring and willing to sacrifice her mental peace for the greater good. She is a homemaker, which, mind you, is no less of a job. She manages the household like a professional and does not allow a single speck of dust to settle down on her furniture. She rarely argues with her partner because she wants to avoid friction. She does not, by such an act, become a weak person but, in fact, it makes her an understanding woman.

The Balanced Woman

The control lies entirely in your hands. You need to infuse this into your personality and character a bit of both the templates illustrated above. It is this balance that will maximize the chances of your relationship working in a smooth manner.

Tips For Introverted Woman

First off lets me start off on a poetic note by saying you are beautiful, unique and designed divinely! Don't you ever forget it! Here is a quote from one of my favorite poets Catalyst C from his book *Memories Tale Of The Broken Collector* ...

"True pristine beauty is drawn from within, derived from the content of your character. Good virtue is far more precious than a ostentation appearance." --Catalyst C

This is incredibly true and so accurate true beauty is incorruptible and is from within. You don't need to feel insecure with the way you look or have a lack of confidence because as the poet Catalyst puts it, your character which is from within is what will reveal and dictate your beauty, and is a pristine beauty that does not perish or corrupt.

Dating has significantly changed with the advent of online dating apps, and most recently mobile dating Tinder, Plenty of Fish, and Tagged just to name a few. The good news is if your introverted in this day and age, that's not a problem!

Through the help of dating apps you can easily match potential dates or even better long term relationships. There is no reason to be single in this day and age! The awkwardness of trying to mingle with someone in person is drastically reduced in regards to your initial contact via "online". Thus, you build rapport and the initial meeting in person won't be so awkward as now you have built some sort of relationship ahead of time. Also, you by this time gained a lot of information on your date and thus have subject matter to converse about when meeting him in person. No excuses ;)

(Back in the day woman had to put themselves out there in person! There was no Tinder, POF or online dating. They had to do things the old fashion way which was a lot harder if you were introverted. But now you have tools, ie: online dating apps, use them!)

Conclusion

Men are genuinely simple creatures to understand. It does not take rocket science to crack what's going on inside a man's brain. We went through the various ways in which a man thinks, acts and behaves. We dived into the deep labyrinths of his mind to figure out the numerous qualities he looks for in a woman. We made ourselves familiar with the importance of distance and trust in a relationship.

Afterward, it was a relationship as a whole that was rummaged and its keystones discovered. Modern day dating was not spared from detailed inspection. There were also tips and tricks provided for single mothers who are searching for a love life once again.

I sincerely hope this book took you through a journey, which at the end you've come out with valuable knowledge, and have become empowered, smarter, and more aware than ever before with regard to how men are when it comes to dating. You now have the blueprint to a man's dating psychology and all you have to do now is implement what you have learnt!

I wish to thank you once again for reading Dating Advice For Women, hope you liked it!

If you thoroughly enjoyed this book would you mind leaving a quality review on Amazon? Please and thank you!

LINK: http://amzn.to/2tiL83T

Good Luck!

www.ingramcontent.com/pod-product-compliance
Lightning Source LLC
Chambersburg PA
CBHW072018290526
45787CB00013B/1287